2

# JOHN ADAMS

*A Life From Beginning to End*

Copyright © 2016 by Hourly History

# Table of Contents

John Adams, the Farmer's Son

John Adams Begins His Career

The Man from Massachusetts

Adams in Philadelphia

Destination Europe

An Experiment in Nationhood

President

A Friendship Restored

# Introduction

John Adams was a passionate husband, married to a wife whose brilliance matched his own at a time when women were expected to be utilitarian and ornamental but not the equal of their spouses. He was ambitious but honest, vain but realistic. He held lofty goals that were often dashed. John Adams, the son of a Massachusetts farmer who, through his own abilities, rose to the highest office of the nation that he helped to create, was evidence that the American experiment was a success.

Adams became proof positive that men (and women, although his wife Abigail's request for him to "remember the ladies" when devising the strategies that would bring about independence did not see results during their lifetimes) who came from ordinary backgrounds could rise as gentlemen of merit rather than birth. It was a concept which the British Empire failed to understand - and it cost them the thirteen colonies.

His years in Philadelphia and in Europe in service to his country meant that Adams and his beloved Abigail endured years of separation. He was often an absent father to his children, and it was Abigail who was the constant figure in their lives. Two sons would be afflicted with a weakness for alcohol; Abigail and John would take care of the widow and children of son Charles, who died of cirrhosis of the liver, and later also care for the children of youngest son Thomas. Their daughter, named for her mother and known as Nabby, died of breast cancer and left her children in her parents' care because her husband was irresponsible. As their grandson, Charles Francis Adams, the son of John Quincy Adams noted, "the history of my family is not a pleasant one to remember. It is one of great triumphs in the world but of deep groans within one of extraordinary brilliancy and deep corroding mortification."

In assessing the achievements of John Adams, the reader is called upon to excavate the essence of the man hidden beneath the layers of political calumny, revolutionary fervor, marital devotion, paternal tragedy, and personal character. John Adams was a complicated man whose accomplishments benefitted the United States of America. When judging him, one must also weigh the results of his acts and decisions. In the end, it is impossible to evaluate the progress of the nation without taking into account the role of this most complicated of Founding Fathers.

# Chapter One

# John Adams, the Farmer's Son

*"I read my eyes out and can't read half enough...the more one reads the more one sees we have to read."*

—John Adams

The sire of America's first political dynasty did not, as a child, appear to exhibit any aspirations which indicated that he had his sights set on prominence. His father, however, was very involved in local government, serving as a Braintree, Massachusetts selectman, constable, and tax collector, as well as a deacon in the Congregational Church. The Adams family, living in what is now Quincy, located fifteen miles south of Boston, consisted of John Adams the father, mother Susanna Boylston Adams, the eldest son John, and two younger brothers, Peter and Elihu. The Adamses came from Puritan stock and had been in the Massachusetts Bay Colony for generations.

Although their founding father was a Puritan, he was not one of the rigid and radical gloomy sect that is typically conjured by the reference. Henry Adams had left England for Massachusetts in 1638, settling near the coast in Braintree to raise a family and live as a farmer. Although little is known about him, he must have possessed some regard for learning because his son, named John, was fond of reading, as was the elder John

Adams' wife, Susanna. It was a passion which they intended to pass on to their eldest son, but John the younger seemed resistant.

As a child of six, the boy was sent to a dame school run by a female named Dalme Belche, where he studied reading, arithmetic, and the tenets of the Protestant religion. However, young John Adams, born October 30, 1735, was more interested in outdoor activities such as hunting than in education, something which troubled his parents, especially when their son took his gun to school so that he didn't have to waste his time returning home but instead could put the time to good use by hunting on the way. There were also times when the boy neglected to go to school at all, preferring to spend his day hunting or fishing.

Hunting was a very good pastime in colonial Massachusetts, but the Adams parents expected more from their eldest son. The Adams family lived a comfortable life but not a wealthy one, and they intended for their son to have a formal education so that, they hoped, he would become a clergyman. When his father asked him what he wanted to do with his life, John Adams, age ten, replied that he wanted to be a farmer, like his father. The elder John Adams obliged, taking his son to the fields to work. His objective was to prove to the boy that farming was hard labor. However, his lesson was wasted; when asked how he liked being a farmer, the boy replied that he liked it very well.

His parents didn't lose sight of their educational goals for their son, however, and they were not raising him to be a farmer. When Adams the son argued that he didn't want to stay in school, his father replied, "You shall comply with my desires." The boy was going to get an education whether he wanted it or not.

Later, he went to the Braintree Latin School, founded by Joseph Cleverly. It offered a preparatory course for young men to ready them for their entrance exams, but still, John Adams disliked the educational process as much as he disliked his schoolmaster. Intent on his son's education, the senior Adams hired a man named Joseph Marsh to prepare his son for the exams. Marsh, who ran a boarding school for boys who lived out of town, was a very different kind of teacher from what Adams had experienced so far, with a broader approach to his work that ignited a love of books and self-discipline in his student. Within a year, Adams was ready for the entrance exams to Harvard.

Adams, at the age of fifteen, enrolled at Harvard College. Thanks to the influence of Marsh, Adams was no longer the lackluster student and was already displaying the signs of his intellectual abilities. He graduated from Harvard in 1755 and delivered a commencement speech which was so impressive that it led to a position at the Central School of Worcester, where the Reverend Thaddeus McCarty hired him to teach grammar school boys and girls.

For Adams, the absence of intellectual stimulation was not compensated by the privilege of training young minds; as he worked, he pondered what his future should be. Should he follow his father's intention and become a clergyman? That path was somewhat compromised by the fact that he was, in terms of Boston philosophy, an unorthodox thinker, not a trait prized in members of the clergy.

The school may not have met his expectations, but he found that Worcester was a pleasant place to live as he met other members of society who appreciated his ability to discuss intellectually challenging ideas. Many of them thought that the law was the best career choice, and James Putnam, a lawyer in the community, welcomed Adams at his side during the Court of Common Pleas of Worcester during Court Week, when area lawyers argued cases. Recognizing that the law would offer the mental stimulation that he relished, Adams settled on becoming a lawyer.

In 1756, he was taken on as an apprentice in the study of law by Putnam, who supervised his studies in the legal profession. This was the traditional method of instruction in the law as it was practiced in Great Britain, although not in Europe, and the British colony had adopted the practice of its homeland. Adams moved in with the Putnams and continued his teaching so that he had an income.

When he was not working, Adams was vigorous in his pursuit of his studies, reading the law books in Putnam's library and using his funds to buy books that Putnam didn't have. That time of study would last for two years, whereupon Adams moved to Braintree. Putnam had failed to swear him in to the Inferior Court of Worcester, so, before being admitted to the Suffolk County bar,

Adams went before several of Boston's best lawyers for the grilling to determine his qualifications for the position.

In May of 1761, John Adams, the father, died in a flu epidemic, leaving his eldest son an inheritance that included property adjoining the family home and seven acres of land that the elder John Adams had purchased in 1720. With land and a career, John Adams had achieved the landmarks of a solid member of the middle class.

The Adams family was known in Massachusetts, and John was not the only Adams of note. Samuel Adams, who would become the first Adams to make himself famous in the colonial quest for independence, was John Adams' second cousin. However, in John Adams' early career, there was no indication of the political fruit that the branches of the Adams family tree would bear. Together, they would change Massachusetts, but it was John Adams who would change the nation.

# Chapter Two

# John Adams Begins His Career

*"It is more important that innocence be protected than it is that guilt be punished, for guilt and crimes are so frequent in this world that they cannot all be punished. But if innocence itself is brought to the bar and condemned, perhaps to die, then the citizen will say, 'whether I do good or whether I do evil is immaterial, for innocence itself is no protection,' and if such an idea as that were to take hold in the mind of the citizen that would be the end of security whatsoever."*

—John Adams

The young lawyer's next hurdle was to establish his practice in Boston, but success did not come quickly. Building up his reputation in the bustling Massachusetts Bay colony took time. His first year as a lawyer yielded a single client; it would take three years before he would win a case in front of a jury. However, perseverance was a trait he had in abundance, and he continued to labor in his field.

Domestic life continued. His mother, a widow since 1761, remarried in 1766 to a military man with whom John Adams did not get along. By then he was already engaged in his own romance with the independent, well-educated Abigail Smith from Weymouth, whose father was a Congregational minister. The Smiths were related to numerous other New England families, and she and John were actually third cousins. Abigail had a high regard for education, studied French, read voraciously, and did not allow her gender or social expectations to limit her capacity to learn. Their romance had evolved unexpectedly.

In 1762, Adams had a friend who was romantically interested in Mary Smith, the older sister of Abigail. Going with him on his romantic errand, John Adams was reacquainted with the fifteen-year-old girl who was as slender as Adams was plump, but their initial attraction was not physical. Adams was, like Abigail, short, but already at age twenty-four, going bald. Adams felt that the Rev. Smith was a crafty, designing man, and Mrs. Smith thought that John Adams ill-mannered.

As business often took Adams into Weymouth, and his friend eventually married Mary Smith, the two came into frequent contact with one another, often enough to spark romantic interest. Abigail Smith, due to her poor health as a child, was kept at home rather than given formal schooling, but in addition to learning how to read and write at home with her mother as her teacher, she had access to the libraries of her father, grandfather, and uncle, an oasis of books on Shakespeare and the classics, philosophy and theology, history and law, and literature. Reading and corresponding with friends occupied most of her leisure time as a young woman. Her education was liberal, but her entertainments were more in keeping with the Puritan tradition, as she did not sing or dance, or play card games.

As the couple discovered more about each other, they realized that each was engrossed in learning. Their letters—the two would prove to be voracious letter writers—reveal a couple comfortable with the physical passion and the intellectual zeal that they shared. They referred to one another in their correspondence as Lysander and Diana, and scattered through the classical references were encouragements to kiss and show affection.

On October 25, 1764, when Abigail was nineteen and John nearly twenty-nine, the couple married, and moved to the small farm in Braintree that John had inherited, riding together on one horse to reach their destination.

Before his marriage, the year 1763 saw Adams begin to flex his media muscles as he published his first articles for newspapers under the name of Humphrey Ploughjogger. His views on the political situation were voiced by a preference for a balance between the institution of democracy, the role of the monarchy, and the position of the aristocracy.

When John and Abigail Adams were born, the colonials were dedicated to their identity as British citizens. However, the smooth fabric of the seam binding the British crown to its colonial subjects was beginning to show signs of fraying. The colonists were well aware that, although they were a rustic and wild country far away from Europe, their fate as a growing collection of independent colonies was closely tied to the Old World's quarrels. In 1763, the French and Indian War, in which the colonial militias fought with the British against the French and their Indian allies, came to an end. The victory meant that Great Britain was truly a world power and the dominant force in North America, but one of the provisions of the war, the one limiting the colonists to expand their territory into the west, was destined to prove a bone of contention for the future.

The Stamp Act, the first direct tax on the colonials, passed in 1765, was bitterly resented for its violation of a principle which inflamed them: taxation without representation. In 1767, the Townsend Acts levied taxes on the sale of paper, tea, lead, and glass. In October of that year, John Adams was given the assignment of drafting the Braintree instructions for the Massachusetts legislature in protest of the Stamp Act. His effective eloquence won adherents, as forty towns adopted the document declaring that taxation without representation was unconstitutional. The belief, passionately held, would before long become a rallying cry.

The colonists resisted with a boycott of the English products; the English merchants depended upon the ready markets of the colonies for their profits, and advocates in London spoke up on behalf of the colonies. The British governing body asserted its right to legislate the laws which governed its colonies when it capitulated and repealed the Stamp Act in 1770, eliminating the taxes. Except, that is, for the tax on tea.

John and Abigail Adams and their two children, daughter Abigail (or Nabby) and son John Quincy, moved to Boston in January of 1768. By then Boston was becoming a center of radical thought; in October of that year, the four thousand soldiers that the governor had requested were sent to the city with the purpose of keeping order. Their assignment was to make sure that taxes were collected, maintain order, and protect the government representatives from the threat of mob violence.

The move to rebellion began gradually. The colonists were infused with a sense of their rights, but to the governing British, those rights came with an acknowledgment of their subordination to the Crown. The British seemed bent upon a course of correction, just as their subjects in the colonies appeared determined to resist. Friction between the Bostonians and the British ignited quickly and stayed hot because they believed that only the Massachusetts Assembly had the right to tax its citizens. Massachusetts voters elected the members of the Assembly. Bostonians were irked that Great Britain, whose Parliament would not have been elected by colonials, could tax the colony.

The colonists, flush with triumph over their victory in the repeal of the Stamp Act, didn't pay much attention to this provision asserting the right of the British overlords to make their colonies behave. They felt that they had won their battle and proven their point. The time had not yet arrived when the Mother Country and her subjects across the ocean would reach a point of irreconcilable differences, and life went on in Boston.

John's days as a struggling lawyer trying to grow his practice proved successful. By 1770, he was recognized as a prominent lawyer with what might have been the largest caseload of any of his fellow Boston attorneys. Adams' clientele included some of the city's most prominent citizens; in 1769, he defended wealthy merchant John Hancock in a wine smuggling charge. Hancock would also come to occupy a prominent place in the move toward independence, but his choice of Adams for his lawyer reflected his confidence in Adams' abilities rather than his political views.

By 1772, Abigail had given birth to five children: Abigail Amelia, John Quincy, Susanna, Charles, and Thomas Boylston. The burden of running the household fell upon Abigail because her husband was away so often, traveling the court circuit and going to other Massachusetts towns. Adams' zeal for his career would be a harbinger of his life as a leader of the revolution when Abigail would spend years on her own while Adams was away. Her son, John Quincy, would later credit his mother's financial acumen and shrewd business sense with keeping the family fortunes thriving as she managed the farm and resources. Abigail was a staunch Patriot, as was her husband, but his dedication to the cause left her alone on the home front with a farm to manage, a family to raise, and a hostile army of occupation in Massachusetts.

## Chapter Three

# The Man from Massachusetts

*"The Part I took in Defence of Cptn. Preston and the Soldiers, procured me Anxiety, and Obloquy enough. It was, however, one of the most gallant, generous, manly and disinterested Actions of my whole Life, and one of the best Pieces of Service I ever rendered my Country. Judgment of Death against those Soldiers would have been as foul a Stain upon this Country as the Executions of the Quakers or Witches, anciently. As the Evidence was, the Verdict of the Jury was exactly right."*

—John Adams

The year 1770 began with grief, as their thirteen-month-old daughter Susanna died in February; Abigail was pregnant at the time with the child that would be her second son, Charles. As usual, private matters and even grief had to step aside for the state dramas which would seize the family, as tragedy had to make way for professional challenges.

March 5th, 1770 was a cold and snowy night, but not too cold for the usual hostility between British soldiers and the Bostonians they were charged with keeping under control. Gathering at the Customs House, Bostonians eager for a fight faced a semicircle of eight soldiers from the Twenty-Ninth regiment and their commanding officer, Captain Thomas Preston. When someone from the crowd struck a soldier with a club, a shot rang out. Then a round of shots was fired, killing five men immediately and wounding two others, one of whom would die nine days later.

The city was outraged. Three weeks later, a grand jury indicted Captain Preston, the soldiers at the Customs House, and four Bostonians who were accused of having fired shots from the Customs House window. The death penalty was their fate if they were found guilty, but when the British soldiers sought a lawyer, they were unsuccessful in their quest; no colonial lawyer wanted to take the case. Adams accepted the case to defend the soldiers even though he risked his professional reputation and the safety of his family, given the mob mentality that frequently held sway over the public at that time. His defense was effective; six of the soldiers were acquitted, and two were charged with manslaughter and branded on the hands, then released. None were executed.

Adams was a firm believer in the right to a fair trial, and that may have been what drove his decision. However, historians speculate that he might also have been influenced by his own ambition. When a seat opened in the Boston legislature three months after the trial ended, John Adams' was Boston's first choice to fill the seat. Was there an agreement? No one knows, but Adams' elected career had begun.

Far from ruining his career, his success in the trial of the Boston Massacre soldiers made him one of Boston's most celebrated lawyers, and he numbered the powerful among his clients. However, his schedule drained him, and as 1771 began, he fell ill from exhaustion. The family chose to move back to Braintree in the spring of 1771, but because his work required him to travel a great deal, a year later, the Adams family returned to Boston.

They would not stay long, however. Boston was a center of the rambunctious Patriot movement, and that meant a hubbub of activity and violence. In 1773, Bostonians were infuriated when the British Parliament passed the Tea Act. This was not actually a new tax. The Tea Act was created so that the British East India Company would have a monopoly on the sale of tea to the colonies. The tax was not onerous; because the Tea Act eliminated the middleman, the tea was available at a lower price than what Bostonians were paying for the tea that they smuggled from the Dutch. However, again, it was taxation without representation. The Sons of Liberty were prepared to both foment dissent and protest the arrival of the tea.

Bostonians dressed in Indian garb boarded the ship to destroy 342 chests of tea that, in today's money, would have been worth more than one million dollars. John Adams was not a player in what would become known as the Boston Tea Party, although he supported it, and he knew that royal punishment would be severe.

It was reason enough for Adams and his family to move back to Braintree, in order to escape the furor the following year. The spring saw the Coercive Acts, or as the colonials described them, the Intolerable Acts, demonstrate that there would be no escaping the wrath of the king, who, determined to teach the rebels a lesson, closed Boston Harbor and installed a royal governor in 1774.

Adams continued to move in political circles, moderating committees and a town meeting, sensing the changing mood of the population. The residents of the other colonies realized that what had happened in Boston could happen in their own colonies and in the fall of 1774, they sent delegates to Philadelphia to meet as the First Continental Congress.

Adams was named as one of the four delegates from Massachusetts. Adams was not a political instigator like his second cousin Sam Adams. In essays published in early 1775, he wrote that the British Parliament had the right to regulate the commerce that took place in the colonies, but it did not have the right to impose taxes upon them. However, Cousin Sam had a far different and much more radical view.

The two men, thirteen years apart in age, with John the junior, shared a great grandfather, Joseph Adams, the son of Henry Adams, who had left Great Britain in 1630 in order to escape the persecution of the Puritans. The family business was malting, but Sam was not suited for it. Nor was he suited to be a tax collector, but it was an advantageous position for a man with political savvy, introducing him to others in the colony who had influence and who shared his views.

Both Sam and John were Harvard graduates, and both studied law. Both served in the Massachusetts House of Representatives, and both represented Massachusetts in the First Continental Congress. However, it was Sam who was the more famous of the two, at least in the beginning of the move to independence; in the eyes of Bostonians, it was Sam Adams who was the political leader. Sam Adams had not been a success in his earlier careers, but he was a first-rate political leader.

He organized the Sons of Liberty, a group known as Patriots—or rebels, depending on which side one stood— who represented different classes from workers to wealthy, but all sharing the dream of independence. It was Sam Adams who kept the colony aware of what was going on, thanks to his Committee of Correspondence.

Sam Adams wold continue to be a figure of influence in Massachusetts, but it was John Adams who would play a role upon the national stage. That drama would begin in Philadelphia.

# Chapter Four

# Adams in Philadelphia

*"Posterity! You will never know how much it cost the
present Generation to preserve your Freedom! I hope you
will make good use of it. If you do not, I shall repent in
Heaven, that I ever took half the Pains to preserve it."*

—John Adams

The Coercive Acts, which were passed by Parliament in
order to make sure that Massachusetts learned its lesson,
alarmed the colonists. They realized that they could not
respond effectively unless they joined forces. A total of
fifty-six delegates from twelve of the thirteen colonies met
in Philadelphia on September 5, 1774. Georgia, because of
its dependence upon the British for help with its Indian
problems, did not send a delegate.

The agenda was simple: boycott British trade; outline
their grievances; and petition the British king and, if the
petition was unsuccessful, convene a Second Continental
Congress. Recognizing the imminent danger, the colonies
agreed that they needed to establish their own militias to
provide protection against the potential threats that
seemed more imminent now that Boston was being
punished.

Well aware that a die had been cast, the Second
Continental Congress met again in Philadelphia in May,

the month after an altercation between British troops and colonial militia, and decided that it needed an army. The eighteenth of April in '75 would a century later, inspire an American poet to turn the political events of Massachusetts into rhyme, but there was nothing poetic about what happened when British soldiers, alerted that there were munitions in the towns of Lexington and Concord, fought with the Massachusetts militia or Minutemen, bringing the opposing forces into armed conflict.

It was a perilous time, but also an exciting one for John Adams. For the New England native who had never traveled beyond his region, Philadelphia was to become an eye-opening experience. When he had attended the First Continental Congress, it was the first time that Adams had the chance to meet colonists from other areas, and he was impressed by what he saw, particularly by the bearing of the Virginian, George Washington. When the Second Continental Congress voted to establish the Continental Army, Adams nominated Washington to serve as commander; the other delegates unanimously agreed.

Philadelphia kept John Adams busy. He would serve the Continental Congress for four years and during that time, he would belong to ninety committees, chairing twenty of them. He was a central figure in the activities of the Congress, but his dedication to the rebel cause meant that he was often away from his home, leaving Abigail to manage the farm and the family in his absence. The two wrote letters and John kept a diary which recorded his thoughts on the birth pangs of the country.

Back in Boston, the war had already begun. In fact, Abigail and son John Quincy could see, from their vantage point in Braintree, the cannon fire as the Battle of Bunker Hill was underway. It was a victory for Great Britain, but a costly one. As yet, John Adams' perspective of the war remained on paper, but he was flattered that his fellow delegates sought him out for his opinions and advice.

Philadelphia's delegates sent the king the Olive Branch Petition, which pledged allegiance to Great Britain and asked the Parliament to end the military action against Boston. Adams opposed the measure, but in the end, it didn't matter, as King George refused to read it.

Adams spent much of the winter of 1775 at home in Braintree, while the port of Boston was under siege. He returned to Philadelphia in February; the British siege ended in March when the troops agreed that they would retreat in peace as long as they were not harmed by the Continental troops.

Mindful of the spirited ideas that were gripping the menfolk in Philadelphia, Abigail got into the act, and she wrote to her husband to remind him to "remember the ladies" when the rights of men were being protected by law. Abigail's reminder to John has a certain poignancy when we think of all the Patriot wives who were keeping homes and families together while their husbands were off doing the manly duty in statesmanship. She warned him in language that indicated her awareness that, just as King George was a tyrant to the American colonists, husbands possessed the same tendency to be tyrannical to their wives. "Do not put such unlimited power into the hands of the Husbands. Remember all Men would be tyrants if they could. That your Sex are Naturally Tyrannical is a Truth so thoroughly established as to admit of no dispute, but such of you as wish to be happy willingly give up the harsh title of Master for the more tender and endearing one of Friend." She predicted that one day, the time would come when the ladies would foment a rebellion of their own and not be "bound by any Laws in which we have no voice, or Representation." No doubt Adams recognized his wife's superlative qualities, although he may not have regarded the rest of her sex as equally able, but the rights of the fair sex did not predominate in the discussion of liberty.

It was a time of daring. John Adams, writing *Thoughts on Government* anonymously, was in favor of a system of government with a legislative, executive, and judicial branch sharing power. He had other committee work as well, serving as the president of the Board of War, a position which was more or less the secretary of war. One of the results of this position was his plan for treaties, which outlined his vision of the alliances between the new country and the nations of Europe. John Adams had his thoughts on the future, but the present day still saw the colonies tied to Great Britain and subject to British authority.

Word reached the colonists in February 1776 that Parliament had passed the Prohibitory Act, which blockaded the ports of the colonies and treated American ships as the enemy. In John Adams' view, Parliament, by doing this, had in effect already declared colonial independence. When the colonists learned that George III was sending German mercenaries to serve in his military and fight the colonists, they were outraged. British punishment, intended to teach the colonists a lesson, was instead angering its subjects.

In March, North Carolina led the way in voting for independence; other colonies followed. In June, Richard Henry Lee of Virginia presented a motion in support of independence. The debate that resulted was intense, as the delegates pondered the potential results of such an act. Was it too soon to declare independence when foreign nations were unlikely to support the country? Some said that foreign countries would not step forward unless the colonies were independent of the Mother Country. Others said that independence already was a fact, and merely needed a declaration from Congress. Not all delegates had the authorization to vote for independence; if the resolution were passed, they said they would leave the Congress.

Congress recognized that a time-out was needed, but not a complete break. The delegates named a committee consisting of John Adams, Thomas Jefferson, Benjamin Franklin, Roger Sherman, and Robert Livingston to draft a document that would officially state the justification for separation from Great Britain. While the committee worked, Congress went on a three-week recess before voting on Lee's resolution.

Recognizing Jefferson's ability to write eloquently, John Adams convinced the committee that it should assign the task of creating the declaration to the Virginian. Adams and Jefferson, by working together, would forge a friendship that would last for decades, until it would suffer from the political ambition which came to mark both men, only to be ultimately revived. However, in 1776, they were advocates for America, and they recognized traits in one another that they prized.

Exhilarated by the document—which was presented to the Congress with only minor edits from Franklin and Adams—Adams wrote to his wife to tell her that July 2, when Congress voted to declare independence from Great Britain, would be "the most memorable epocha in the history of America." He was off by two days: July 4, 1776, the day when the Declaration of Independence was signed, became the birthdate of the new nation, the United States of America.

# Chapter Five

# Destination Europe

*"As much as I converse with sages and heroes, they have very little of my love and admiration. I long for rural and domestic scene, for the warbling of birds and the prattling of my children."*

—John Adams

That the marriage of John and Abigail Adams was so strong and loving is a testimonial to the character of the pair. Except for comparatively brief visits back to Braintree, John Adams was serving his country with far more dedication than he served his family during the years of revolution. While he was working on the lofty goal of creating a nation, Abigail had to contend with the mundane challenges of daily living. She oversaw the education of the Adams children. She was the one who had the household inoculated against smallpox. She took care of the farming. She spun and wove fabric so that the family would have clothing after the non-importation acts prevented the Patriots from using textiles imported from Great Britain. She was wife and mother, daughter and sister-in-law, juggling many obligations and concerns. In 1775, Abigail's mother and John's brother died from an outbreak of dysentery, but John was in Philadelphia, serving on committees and planning to midwife a nation.

In July 1777, just a month after the Second Continental Congress designed the flag that would serve as the nation's symbol, Abigail Adams delivered a stillborn daughter. Her loss was no doubt magnified by fear when September came and the British captured Philadelphia; fortunately, her husband and the Congress had escaped to York, Pennsylvania. The end of the year saw the Congress adopt the Articles of Confederation, a weak and clumsy attempt to create a system of governing which saw the individual states, colonies no longer, responsible for coining their own currency and their own judicial and legislative systems. John Adams returned home to his family and his law practice in November, but again, his stay in Braintree would be short-lived; in February 1778, he sailed to serve as a commissioner to France, which had allied itself with the new country and entered the war on the Americans' behalf. This time, he took his oldest son, ten-year-old John Quincy, with him. He had intended to take his entire family but sea travel, never comfortable, was particularly dangerous for a man whose life was sought by the mighty British Empire. The crossing took six weeks, but when he arrived in France, he discovered that Benjamin Franklin and Arthur Lee had already negotiated an agreement with Paris. Ever the organizer, Adams turned his attention to making sense out of the paperwork that needed attending to and paying heed to the finances of the delegation. There were diplomatic tasks as well, including exchanging prisoners of war and dealing with confrontations between pirates and American merchants.

While Franklin, that shrewd and deceptively homespun man of the world, was a favorite of the French, John Adams was the out-of-place Yankee with his stern morals and lack of finesse. A year and a half after his arrival, Congress named Franklin as the single minister to the country, and John Adams was obliged to return home with a sense that he had not been appreciated for his efforts.

But France's loss was Massachusetts' gain. Once home again, Adams drafted the Massachusetts Constitution of 1780, a document destined to have an influence on the yet-to-be-written Constitution which would eventually establish the country's governing structure.

It's to be hoped that Abigail enjoyed having her family intact once more, because, in November of 1779, Adams left again to cross the ocean to negotiate the terms of peace with Great Britain. The war was not yet over, and Adams realized that success was dubious. Congress knew what it wanted—access to the land west of the Mississippi River and south to the thirty-first parallel and the south of Canada, and the fisheries of Newfoundland, as well as an agreement for future trade with the British. The French were alarmed by this threat of a thaw, and Adams had to agree to a treaty which stated that the war would only conclude when all the allies agreed that it was over.

Adams was no Francophile and believed that Franklin was too fond of the French to be an effective negotiator. The French negotiator disliked his American counterpart and communicated his thoughts to the American

Congress, criticizing Adams as not being suited for the assignment.

However, Congress continued to put him to use, sending him in July of 1780 to negotiate with the Dutch. The Netherlands was less eager to enter into a trade agreement, and they were not enthusiastic at Adams' request for a loan that would buttress American efforts to be less dependent upon the French. Adams, however, was persistent. That, combined with the American victory at Yorktown in 1781, persuaded the Dutch that the Americans just might make it, and they agreed to a two million dollar loan. With Dutch funds, a military turn of luck, and the British surrender up his sleeve, Adams returned to Paris with more leverage in 1782 as he was assigned the task of negotiating the preliminary treaty between the two nations.

In 1783, he, Franklin, and John Jay would sign the Treaty of Paris that ended the long war of independence. After negotiating a second loan with the Dutch in 1784 at the beginning of the year, the Adams family reunited, but not in Massachusetts. Abigail and daughter Nabby spent a month sailing the Atlantic and arrived in London in August; John Adams had not seen his wife and daughter for five years. Abigail suffered from sea sicknesses and for sixteen days was too ill to record her thoughts on paper, an unheard-of length of time for the communicative Mrs. Adams.

When Adams was named the American minister to Great Britain, Abigail went from being a Massachusetts housewife to the wife of the first American minister to

Great Britain, moving to London and living in the American embassy. John Adams had an audience with the King, and Abigail and her daughter were presented to the Queen. The French Revolution, which turned the streets of Paris into a bloodbath wrought alarm across Europe, and there was a belief that the English monarchy could be in jeopardy. However, the royal couple did not conceal their distaste for the Americans, and Abigail wrote that she felt compassion for the English but not for Queen Charlotte and that she would not be sympathetic if the queen suffered humiliation. "Humiliation for Charlotte," Abigail wrote, "is no sorrow for me; she richly deserves her full portion for the contempt and scorn which she took pains to discover."

In 1784, Thomas Jefferson was sent to serve as a diplomat to France, and the two Americans enjoyed renewing their friendship, becoming friends with Abigail as well. Abigail described Jefferson as "one of the choice ones of the earth." Jefferson told his fellow Virginian James Madison that Adams was "so amiable that I pronounce you will love him if you ever become acquainted with him." Adams, who would become well known for his inability to get along with others, told Jefferson that ""intimate Correspondence with you … is one of the most agreable Events in my Life."

They did some sightseeing, touring English gardens and stopping at the home of William Shakespeare, where they took a piece from the chair that had belonged to the Bard for a souvenir in accordance, Adams said, with the custom. Their six-day tour in a hired coach brought them to Blenheim Palace and the University of Oxford. However, this spirit of friendship was destined not to survive the test of political gain when both men returned from Europe and pursued careers which would turn them into bitter rivals.

# Chapter Six

# An Experiment in Nationhood

*"My country in its wisdom contrived for me the most insignificant office that ever the invention of man contrived or his imagination conceived."*

—John Adams

The men who fought in the Revolution tend to be seen as haloed, hallowed heroes who forged a nation out of ideals, spilled blood, and the knowledge borne out of the Enlightenment. However, when the Patriots left the battlefield, the gloves came off. The cast of characters in those early years exhibited a level of ruthless partisanship that makes modern-day machinations pale in comparison.

John Adams, equal to all of the other men who would become known as the Founding Fathers, had served his country as a diplomat in Europe for a decade. It was time to return home and gauge his political future. It was an uncertain time; he had to decide whether he had a role to play in the nation's destiny or whether he was better off returning to Massachusetts to return to the law.

He came back as a man well regarded by a nation that appreciated his service and that inspired him to run for the office of the president along with candidates John Hancock, the Massachusetts merchant, and George

Washington, the victorious general. Washington, with sixty-nine electoral votes, became president, to no one's surprise, and John Adams, who received the second greatest number of votes with thirty-four electoral votes, was his vice president. Hancock, a regional candidate, only received four votes.

Adams was disappointed by the limited powers of his office, to which he was re-elected for Washington's second term. However, as vice president, he was influential by casting the tie-breaking vote in approximately thirty votes in his role as leader of the Senate; those votes included deciding where to locate the national capital, defending the President's right to remove Senate appointees, and avoiding a second war with Great Britain.

George Washington, the pragmatist, was committed to a governing process which did not fracture into divisive political parties. It was not long before Washington's forlorn hope became a failed dream. Nonetheless, Washington deserves credit for some of the innovations that he brought to the presidency: he served as president for two terms and then returned to civilian life, a pattern which other presidents followed until Franklin Roosevelt in 1940; and he began the tradition of naming advisors to his Cabinet so that he could benefit from expert advice in areas where he needed insights: Thomas Jefferson as Secretary of State and Alexander Hamilton as Secretary of the Treasury are the two most notable appointees. It was those two men, one a Virginian, one a New Yorker, who initiated the political parties which opposed one another and created a hostile landscape.

Thomas Jefferson, the Southerner and founder of the Democratic-Republican Party, favored a weak central government with the power coming from the individual states. He and other planters, the elite of their states, believed in an agricultural economic system. John Adams and Alexander Hamilton, Federalists, believed that in order for the United States to thrive, the central government needed to be strong. The cohesiveness which had given President Washington a consensus was not destined to last.

Washington did not plan to seek a third term. The Federalist Party nominated John Adams and Thomas Pinckney as presidential candidates. The Democratic-Republicans chose Thomas Jefferson and Aaron Burr. The electoral process, which was finally honed when the 12th amendment to the Constitution was ratified, allowed each elector to vote for two persons, but not by the separate offices of president and vice president. Whoever won the most votes became the president; the person with the second highest tally of votes was then the vice president. This was why parties had multiples candidates for the same office, with the aim of success for one of them.

The decision to nominate and elect George Washington as the nation's first president was an easy one. Who else but Washington deserved and could perform the inauguration of the great American experiment in democracy? However, the naiveté was gone by the election of 1796, and the neophytes had learned that ideals were all well and good but campaigning called for tougher measures.

And campaign they did. The Democratic-Republicans promoted Thomas Jefferson and his views while the Federalists did the same for Washington's Vice President, John Adams. The events in France appeared bloody and horrific even for a nation which had just rejected a monarch, albeit without a guillotine to do the dirty work, and the Federalists capitalized on the reaction by connecting Jefferson and his party with the mob rule and anarchy of the French Revolution.

For their part, the Democratic-Republicans made the volatile claim that the Federalists supported England and were proponents of the monarchy and the elite, and favored a strong central government which threatened the power of the individual states. The Federalists were lambasted for Jay's Treaty, which Alexander Hamilton had crafted and which smoothed some of the remaining rough edges which had not been addressed in the Treaty of Paris ending the American Revolution. Relations between the British and Americans still had tense moments, but Jay's Treaty, so named because it was negotiated by John Jay, included the British Army's withdrawal from forts it had established before the Revolution in the Northwest Territory. Items of contention such as the boundary between the United States and Canada were sent to arbitration. The treaty also covered trade concerns, but the Jeffersonians saw the treaty as evidence that the Americans were cozying up to their former masters, the British. The French, unaware or uncaring that it was impolitic for a foreign nation to involve itself in the campaign, voiced support for

Jefferson, thereby creating embarrassment for the Democratic Republicans, which were also dealing with the attacks made by the Federalists on Jefferson's moral character, accusing him of being an atheist and a coward.

It didn't help that Federalist Alexander Hamilton, who was not as moderate as Adams, was working against Adams. Hamilton supported Pinckney over Adams and persuaded the South Carolina electors to cast their second votes for their governor. This ploy only exacerbated the hostility between Hamilton and Adams.

This election was the sole time in American history when the president and vice president represented different political parties. Although there have certainly been eras when presidents and their vice presidents were less than cordial, it's unlikely that any faced the situation of Adams and Jefferson. As vice president, Jefferson exploited his office to plan his campaign for the election of 1800, opposing Adams' policies and laying the groundwork for a future election with an outcome more favorable to his ambition.

# Chapter Seven

# President

*"I'm obnoxious and disliked, you know that, sir."*

—Lyrics from *1776*, the Broadway musical

As president of the Senate, it fell to John Adams to tally the votes of the election results. The winner was … John Adams, who had seventy votes, including all the votes from New England; Thomas Jefferson was second, making him vice president, with sixty-eight votes cast by strong support from the South.

Abigail, having spent so much time in Europe at foreign courts, had been able to help the President's wife in entertaining during Washington's terms in office and had built a friendship with Martha Washington, but she began to suffer from ill health in 1791, which frequently sent her back home to Massachusetts. Adams missed her, not just out of his love for her but also because he needed her advice, and he wanted her to return to join him when he was elected to the presidency in 1797. "I never wanted your Advice and assistance more in my life. The Times are critical and dangerous, and I must have you here to assist me." However, Abigail, who was taking care of her dying mother-in-law, could not attend her husband's presidential inauguration.

Although she loathed Philadelphia, she returned in the spring of 1797 to join her husband. She recognized that the presidency would change their lives and wrote that she regretted the "envy, hatred, malice and all uncharitableness" that she saw evident in the government. Abigail, who relished candor and forthright speech, described being the president's wife as " *fastened up hand and foot and tongue to be shot at as our Quincy lads do at the poor geese and turkies." She wondered how she would be able to take the necessary vow of silence that was required in order to avoid controversy.*

*Controversy was inevitable.* Adams was expected to maintain Washington's policies. The merchants and industrialists were confident that he would represent them. Adams had a solid reputation and more experience in foreign affairs than any other of the candidates, and he expected to be able to focus on international matters while Congress addressed the national agenda. His international experience made him turn to his own family, as he named son John Quincy to serve the country as the minister to Prussia, an assignment which made his son uneasy, fearing that the family connection would lead to charges of nepotism.

Unfortunately, John Adams' own nature was his biggest enemy. He could not bring about accord within the government, even within his own Cabinet. He did not have confidence in public opinion, and his own Federalist Party was split between Adams' moderate faction and the conservative wing, which was led by Alexander Hamilton.

Almost immediately, Adams faced an international dilemma with America's former ally, France, which had its roots in the Washington administration. The French resented Jay's Treaty because, in their view, it failed to honor the previous treaties signed by France and the United States. Adams sent a delegation to Paris in 1797 to meet with French Foreign Minister Talleyrand. Talleyrand's agents explained that in order to meet, Talleyrand first required a substantial bribe of $250,000 for himself and a $12 million loan for France. Bribery was commonplace among diplomatic circles at the time, but the amounts were regarded as excessive; Americans, upon learning of the outrageous conditions, cried out for war. When Adams showed the members of Congress the reports from the American diplomats, he replaced the names of the French agents with the letters X, Y, and Z, from which the episode took its name. Congress did not authorize war, but it did take measures to defend the country, including the establishment of the Department of the Navy. Warships were built and, in 1798, American ships were given permission to attack French ships. The resulting naval conflict was called the Quasi-War.

What was an international problem turned into a political advantage for the Federalists, who perceived that they could turn the anti-French sentiment in the country to their own use for the next election. The Alien and Sedition Acts, passed in 1798, were ostensibly designed to protect America's foreign policy by preventing anyone in the country from assisting France. However, there were deeper roots to the legislation as the Acts, which consisted of four parts, including a segment targeting immigrants who generally voted for candidates of the Democratic-Republican Party. Under the Naturalization Act, the period of residency before an immigrant could become a citizen was extended from five years to fourteen years. The Alien Act, which was supported by both parties, allowed enemy aliens in the country to be detained without a trial. The Alien Enemies Act gave the president the power to deport aliens who were regarded as threats to national security. The Sedition Act punished speech deemed subversive to national security with fines and prison terms. Although there were fifteen indictments and ten convictions under the Sedition Act, no one was deported. However, it had an adverse effect on immigrants who had come to the United States, and hundreds left the country in 1798 and 1799.

Ultimately, the effect of the Alien and Sedition Acts was to empower the Democratic-Republicans as the defenders of liberty against governmental tyranny.

Finally, in November of 1800, Adams' most trusted advisor, his wife, arrived in the nation's capital of Washington D.C. The President's House was as raw and unfinished as the capital, which had few paved streets. In order to obtain water, the servants had to walk five blocks away. With no sufficient laundry accommodations, the wife of the president had to improvise. "We had not the least fence, yard or other convenience without, and the great unfinished audience room, I made a drying room of—nor were there enough lusters or lamps, so candles were stuck here and there for light." The main staircase and outer steps were incomplete, requiring the Adamses to come into the White House via temporary stairs and a platform. But she met her social obligations as the wife of the president, holding Monday night receptions for everyone and Wednesday evening formal dinners.

The Adams' would not have to endure the privations of Washington D.C. for much longer. The looming election of 1800 was poised to become one of the most bitter that the nation would ever endure. Both the Federalists and the Democratic-Republicans fervently believed that their opponents were threats to the wellbeing of the nation. Thomas Jefferson and Aaron Burr were the opponents of the incumbent President John Adams and his running mate Charles Pinckney. The rhetoric which had been employed in the 1796 election was even more vitriolic. Jefferson, said the Federalists, would import the chaos of the French Revolution to America. Jefferson was a strong supporter of the separation of church and state; therefore, said the Federalists, he was an atheist. Adams, countered the Democratic-Republicans, wanted to establish a central government so strong that it would crush the states. The Alien and Sedition Acts were unpopular, as were the taxes that had been levied to expand the American military. These issues gave the Democratic-Republicans the edge in popularity.

However, it was the Electoral College which would make the decision. When the ballots were counted, the result was a tie between the Federalists' John Adams and Charles Pinckney and the Democratic-Republican Party's

Thomas Jefferson and Aaron Burr. The Constitution, which failed to distinguish between votes for the two offices, held that when an election resulted in a tie, the House of Representatives would make the decision. If the election wasn't already controversial, it was about to get even more so. The Federalists were still in power in the lame-duck session of Congress; they wanted to defeat Jefferson, so they supported Burr. Alexander Hamilton, once again pulling puppet strings behind the scenes, detested Burr and worked to get Federalists to support Jefferson. Burr claimed to support Jefferson but was angling to win the office for himself.

After thirty-six ballots had been cast, Thomas Jefferson was finally named the winner, with Aaron Burr as his vice president.

It was an election with consequences. But perhaps the most significant one was the fact that power was peacefully handed over from the sitting president to his opponent, with no threat to the government. The experiment in democracy, regardless of how bruised and battered it was, worked.

# Conclusion

# A Friendship Restored

*"Of the two great political parties which have divided the opinions and feelings of our country, the candid and the just will now admit that both have contributed splendid talents, spotless integrity, ardent patriotism, and disinterested sacrifices to the formation and administration of this Government, and that both have required a liberal indulgence for a portion of human infirmity and error."*

—John Quincy Adams

After John Adams was defeated in the election of 1800, he returned home to Massachusetts and the family farm. It was because of his wife's adroit management of the farm that had allowed John Adams to pursue his political ambitions, and it was thanks to her skilled handling that there was a home to return to and income from what she had saved. There was no pension for former presidents, so there would have been no income if not for Abigail's stewardship. While he was busy with the Continental Congress, John Adams had admitted, perhaps in jest, that he had received word that the family far had never looked better than it did under his wife's management.

Abigail Adams had an advantage over many of her female contemporaries. She could look back on a life of influence, confident that she had been of service to her country. It was a tribute to her own innate abilities, but also the dedication of her husband; whatever his personal faults, he was devoted to his wife. Their loyalty to the nation was passed on to their children and subsequent generations, as the Adams progeny would serve as presidents, ambassadors, and writers.

In 1814, Abigail wrote to her granddaughter, "Yesterday completes half a century since I entered the marriage state, then just your age. I have great cause of thankfulness that I have lived so long and enjoyed so large a portion of happiness as has been my lot. The greatest source of unhappiness I have known in that period has arisen from the long and cruel separations which I was called, in a time of war, and with a young family around me, to submit to."

When she was seventy-three years old, she died of typhoid fever in 1818. She did not live long enough to see son John Quincy elected as the sixth president in the controversial election which was decided by the House of Representatives.

John Adams outlived his wife by eight years. They had endured much as spouses and parents, climbing great heights of achievement and enduring overwhelming lows both professionally and personally. Two sons, Charles and Thomas, died from their alcoholism; daughter Nabby died of breast cancer. Abigail and John were left to care for a widowed daughter-in-law and grandchildren.

Despite the challenges and the loss in 1818 of his wife, John Adams lived long enough to see a treasured friendship restored to him. Following the bitter election of 1800, John Adams and Thomas Jefferson, political rivals turned enemies, witnessed the abandonment of their friendship. In 1809, after Jefferson left Washington D.C. upon the conclusion of his second term as president, another signer of the Declaration of Independence, Dr. Benjamin Rush, decided that it was time for the two men to reconcile. His efforts seemed doomed to failure until a neighbor of Thomas Jefferson visited John Adams in 1811. Upon returning to Virginia, the neighbor told Jefferson that Adams had said that he always had, and continued to love, Thomas Jefferson. Rush received a letter from Jefferson, which stated, "This is enough for me. I only needed this knowledge to revive towards him all of the affections of the most cordial moments of our lives." Rush contacted Adams with the information and Adams responded with a letter to Jefferson. The years of silence were forgotten, and both men resumed their correspondence, sharing their thoughts on the political scene in the country, religion, philosophy, even aging. Spanning five decades, the correspondence between the two men included 380 letters that showed the rich history of two men who had given so much to their country.

They would die on the same day in 1826, on a date which was a tribute to their lives and which became a commemoration of their deaths. On July 4, 1826, the fiftieth anniversary of the signing of the Declaration of Independence, Thomas Jefferson breathed his last. Unaware that Jefferson was gone, John Adams, on his deathbed, spoke his last words: "Thomas Jefferson survives."

Both men played an integral role in the formation of the nation, but John Adams are too often seen as a lesser figure than the mighty giants of Washington and Jefferson. Biographer and award-winning historian David McCullough is of the opinion that few men contributed more than John Adams did to the birth of the United States of America. His presidency, when viewed through the prism of the Alien and Sedition Acts, is viewed as a failure, and it's true that these acts reflected badly on him and the nation, but Adams was a complicated man who accomplished great deeds on behalf of his nation, and he can't be judged solely by his errors.

His decision to defend the soldiers charged in the Boston Massacre was a professional choice that revealed a man whose devotion to the law was stronger than his own political views. A nation with such a man as one of its leaders could be confident in receiving a just compass for leadership. His writings outlined the course of freedom that navigated the colonies into nationhood. As a president, he avoided war, using negotiation and the strength of convictions to secure peace with honor. He helped to nurture the strength of a government which had no example upon which to model itself. He was often irascible and irritable, but he was honest and steadfast as well.

When Adams moved into the newly built but not-yet-finished president's house which would become the White House, he wrote in a letter to Abigail his wish that, "I pray Heaven to bestow the best of Blessings on this House and all that shall hereafter inhabit it. May none but honest and wise Men ever rule under this roof."

Not even the most fervent idealist could claim that his prayers were answered. However, what can be claimed is that the second president of the United States was personally honest, morally steadfast, and politically committed to the best and brightest aspirations of the new nation he helped to create.

Made in United States
Troutdale, OR
08/13/2023

12060328R00030